Max and Bertie Bring Back Bees

Copyright © 2015 Nicola Gothard

All rights reserved

ISBN: 978-0-9931527-3-3

Published by Generation 2050

www.generation2050project.org

It was a rainy day in London where Max was splishing and splashing in the puddles as he walked home from school. He was carrying an umbrella decorated in colourful flowers.

Suddenly, Max heard a loud thud
and then a 'Bzzzzzz'

'Ahhhhh!' screamed Max
'Bzzzaahhhh!' a little voice buzzed back at him.

Max quickly threw his umbrella to the ground and backed away.

Then he saw it, all black and yellow fuzzy fur with big bulging eyes - a bumblebee.

He looks sad and tired, thought Max.

'Are you ok?' Max whispered.
'I'm hungry, where are all the flowers?' Said the bee.
'This is London, it's a city! We don't have many flowers. Do you eat flowers?' asked Max.

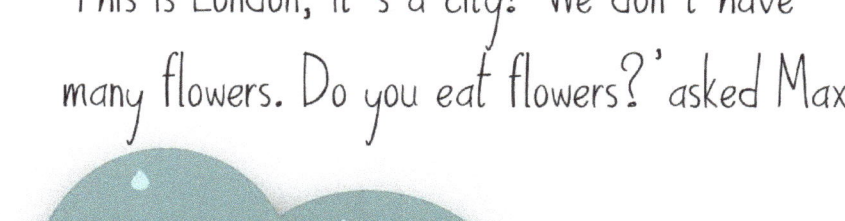

'I drink the nectar from flowers.'
'What's **nectar**?'
'It's a yummy sweet drink' said the bumblebee.

Max's eyes lit up. He had an idea to help the bumblebee.
He opened up his lunch box and took out his orange juice.
'Here have this, it's sweet and yummy too.'

The tired bumblebee crawled on to Max's open hand
and began to drink the juice. He unfolded his long hairy
tongue called a **Proboscis** and sucked up the juice as if he were using a straw.

Once the bee had lapped up all the juice he bounced in to the sky and zoomed around before coming back down to Earth to thank Max.

'My name is Bertie,' said the bumblebee.
'I'm Max.'
'Thank you for the juice Max. I feel much better now,' said Bertie bee.
'I'm glad you liked it Bertie.
Where are the flowerzzz Max?' buzzed Bertie.

'Most of the flowers are in the wild. You should go to the wild Bertie.'
'I can't,' said Bertie.
'Why?'

'I used to live in the wildflower meadows but the builders came and built houses.'

'Then I moved to the farm but the farmers don't like bugs eating their crops so they spray them with poison called **pesticide** to make bugs sick.'

'So I came to the city to see if I could find a home here but I can't find any flowers,' Bertie sighed.

'Bertie, I know what to do. I will grow some flowers for you,' said Max excitedly.

Max and Bertie raced back to Max's home as fast as they could.

Max told his Mummy about Bertie's problem and together they looked on the internet for the best wildflowers to feed bumblebees like Bertie.

They learnt that bumblebees enjoy sipping the nectar of over 200 types of wildflowers including lavender, honeysuckle and strange sounding plants like Vipers Bugloss.

Max and his Mummy went to the shops and bought boxes and boxes of wildflower seeds.

They also got a lavender plant for Bertie to snack on whilst they waited for the flowers to grow.

The children rode their bikes and threw seeds in to the wind as they went by.

They went to the city parks and planted wildflowers there too.

They planted flowers and seeds along all the grassy verges they could find in the city.

Max asked a shopkeeper if he could plant flowers outside his shop but the shopkeeper was worried about bees stinging his customers.

Bertie told Max that bees only sting when people get too close and scare them. Max told the shopkeeper that bees are **pollinators** and have a very important job to do called **pollination**. They help the plants we eat to grow by moving **Pollen** from plant to plant.

As the summer passed, the sun shone and the rain came.
Soon the flowers started to bloom.

The city had never looked so colourful.
The bright flowers sparkled and more bees
came to drink the nectar.
Bertie was happy to have more bees to play with.

Bertie and his bee friends built a beehive outside Max's home so he would never be far away.

'Thank you for helping the bees Max, you are a good friend,' said Bertie.

'Thank you for making the city come to life Bertie. It was grey and smelly and now it's colourful and smells so lovely.'

Glossary

- **Pesticide** - A pesticide is a chemical used to kill pests. Pests are animals that people don't like.

- **Proboscis** - A Proboscis is a bees straw-like tongue which it uses to drink nectar.

- **Pollen** - Pollen is a sticky yellow powder from flowers that pollinators carry between plants.

- **Pollinator** - Pollinators are animals that carry the pollen of flowering plants from one plant to another. Pollinators include insects such as ants, beetles, butterflies and moths as well as other animals such as birds and bats.

Pollination - Pollination is how plants make new plants. Pollination happens when the pollen from one plant is taken to another plant by a pollinator and joins with an egg to make a seed.

Nectar - Nectar is a sweet food made by plants to attract pollinators.

Seed - Plants make seeds when egg cells are pollinated. Seeds carry the beginnings of new plants inside them. If you plant seeds in the ground, new plants can grow.

WWW.GENERATION2050PROJECT.ORG

PLANET   PEOPLE   ANIMALS

Generation 2050 is a social enterprise which publishes ethical childrens stories and educational materials to encourage and inspire a generation of socially and environmentally conscious citizens.

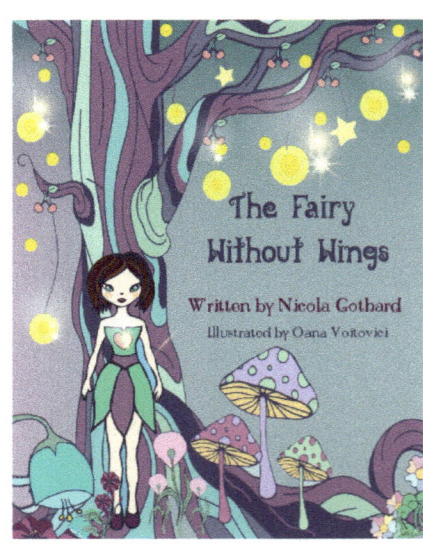

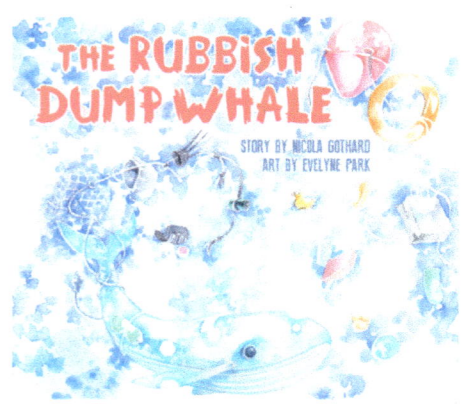

If you enjoyed this story please pass it on and check out our other titles available in both ebook and print formats from most major online book retailers.

@GEN2050

www.ingramcontent.com/pod-product-compliance
Lightning Source LLC
Chambersburg PA
CBHW061933290426